THE PUZZLE EMPORIUM

PRESENTS

MIND BENDING CONUNDRUMS

THIS IS A CARLTON BOOK

This edition published in 2013
by Carlton Books Limited
20 Mortimer Street
London W1T 3JW

ISBN 978-1-78097-316-6

10 9 8 7 6 5 4 3 2 1

Printed and bound in Great Britain by CPI Group (UK) Ltd, Croydon CR0 4YY

THE PUZZLE EMPORIUM
PRESENTS

MIND
BENDING
CONUNDRUMS

CARLTON
BOOKS

Contents

Welcome to the Puzzle Emporium ...

If you're looking to expand your mind and blow the dust off your brain cells, you've come to the right place. Roll up, ladies and gentlemen. Roll up your selves and your sleeves, and get stuck in to the most thrilling collections of brain teasers, conundrums and enigmas ever to grace the pages of this (and possibly any other) book. The Puzzle Emporium is a carnival of wonders and delights all specially designed to cater to your every mental whim.

Puzzles and riddles are as old as humanity. In every culture we know, there is evidence for recreational mental challenges, from the smallest, most isolated Amazon tribes down through the mists of time to the ancient societies of Sumeria and Babylonia.

To puzzle, ladies and gentlemen, is to be human.

But it's not just fun and games. There's a serious side. Our curiosity, our need to find out how things work, is the driving force behind social evolution. Without our mental ambition, none of this would ever have happened.

It's just as important on a personal level, too. Research has proven beyond doubt that "Use it or lose it" is not just for physical muscles. If you want to keep your mind sharp, you need to give it some lifting to do. Luckily, that's fun at the same time.

So dig in. Enjoy our puzzles. And reconnect with what it means to be human.

PUZZLES

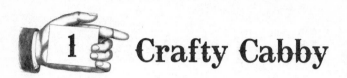

1 Crafty Cabby

In his book *Aha! Insight*, master gamesman Martin Gardner tells the story of a talkative, highly-strung woman who hailed a taxicab in New York City.

During the journey, the lady talked so much that the taxi driver got quite annoyed. He said, "I'm sorry lady, but I can't hear a word you're saying. I'm deaf as a post, and my hearing aid isn't working today." On hearing this, the lady stopped talking, but after she had left the cab she realized that the cabby had lied to her. How did she know?

2 Insomnia

IBM executives held a convention in Miami. John and Edgar occupied two interconnecting rooms, numbers 518 and 519 at the Fontainebleu Hotel.

After a strenuous day of lectures and partying, they went to their rooms. Edgar, in spite of being exhausted, could not fall asleep. He tossed and turned without avail. Finally, at 2 am, he phoned the operator and asked to be connected with John's room. As soon as John answered the telephone, Edgar replaced the receiver and fell asleep.

Explain!

3 How Did He Die

A dead man was found hanging from a chandelier in a sealed room. There was a puddle of water on the floor beneath his feet. All the doors and windows were locked from the outside. The man was alone and the room was empty of furniture or other items.

How did the man die?

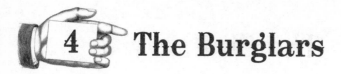

4 ☞ The Burglars

John lives with his parents in a large flat in north London. One afternoon, while his parents were out, John was sitting on the sofa with Sophie, the neighbours' daughter, watching television. After a short while, Sophie left to buy some cigarettes. Suddenly two men burst into the flat and, ignoring John, proceeded to take the television set, a tape recorder and a PC and disappeared.

John had never seen either of the men before, nor was there any legal reason for them to remove the equipment, yet he remained sitting on the sofa throughout the incident without taking any action.

Explain.

The Birthday

Alice and George were window shopping in London's Bond Street. As they passed a jeweller, Alice stopped and admired a bracelet, one of three, with the motif of a leopard silhouetted in semi-precious stones.

George, reading her mind: "Darling, I would love to make this your birthday present, but it must be far beyond my budget."

"Let's ask, just for fun," ventured Alice, and they entered the shop.

The salesman fetched the bracelet from the window. Alice tried it on and looked pleadingly at her husband. Asked for the price, the salesman hesitated for a brief moment: "£250 for payment in cash." George could not hide his surprise, as the piece looked more like £3-5,000. "The stones are paste," volunteered the salesman by way of explanation, and he offered to reserve the bracelet until George would return with the cash.

The following day, Alice waited impatiently for George's return. When he opened the door she noticed a smug smile on his face: "Darling, you won't believe this, but when I showed the bracelet to Oscar, the jeweller in Swiss Cottage, he offered me £800. I can now buy you all three and still be left with a profit." Alice was near tears when she recovered from her shock. "No, George, I have changed my mind, I don't want another bracelet. In fact I don't want any birthday present, thank you."

Explain.

6 Death In Squaw Valley

A New York banker and his wife took their annual skiing vacation in the Valley.

Late one afternoon, in bad visibility, the wife skidded over a precipice and broke her neck. The coroner returned a verdict of accidental death and released the body for burial.

In New York an airline clerk read about the accident. He contacted the police and gave them some information which resulted in the husband's arrest and indictment for first degree murder. The clerk did not know the banker nor his wife.

Explain.

7 Happy and Sad

Three women are standing together. Each one wears a swimming costume. Two women are sad and one is happy. Both the sad women are smiling, and the happy one is weeping.

Explain.

The Sharpshooter

A sharpshooter hung up his hat and put on a blindfold. He then walked 100 yards, turned around, and shot a bullet through his hat. The blindfold was a perfectly good one and completely blocked the man's vision. How did he manage this feat?

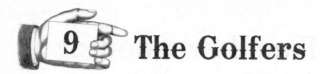

9 The Golfers

Sidney and Stanley were professional golfers and keen rivals. They were playing a game in which each had scored 30 points. Stanley then hit a bad shot, whereupon Sidney immediately added 10 points to his own score. Sidney then hit a good shot and won the game.

Explain.

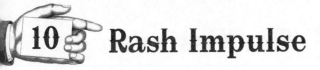

10 Rash Impulse

A man stood looking through the window on the tenth floor of a block of flats.

On a sudden impulse, he opened the window and jumped. There was no balcony and it was a sheer drop to the ground, and yet the man landed quite unhurt. He did not use a parachute, nor did he land in water or on any special soft surface.

Explain.

11 Staying Dry

Five brothers were walking home together down a country lane when it began to rain. Four of the men began to walk faster. The fifth did not alter his pace but he remained dry while the other four all got wet. They all arrived at their destination at the same time. No means of transport other than by foot was used.

Explain.

12 The Kiss

A young woman approached a stranger in the street, and, without either of them saying a word, kissed him on the lips. It was the middle of the morning, and the woman had never seen the man before nor did she know who he was. She was not attracted to him, and her actions were not prompted by the possibility of obtaining a reward of any kind.

Why did she do it?

13 Mass Murder?

A man lived alone for eight weeks, during which time no-one visited him and he never left the house. Eventually he went mad, and one night he put out the fire, turned off the lights, and walked out of the house never to be seen or heard of again. His actions that night resulted in the deaths of 142 people.

How come?

14 Communication Problem

A man and his two daughters were having dinner together in a restaurant. The man spoke to each of his daughters, and each of them replied to him, but the daughters never spoke to each other. They had not quarrelled and did not dislike each other, but they never addressed a word to one another. Explain.

15 Being Neighbourly

Davina and Jeremy were a young, active couple who lived next door to Arthur, a 92-year old invalid. One day, Davina asked Arthur to come over to her house to do some paperwork which neither she nor Jeremy could do. There was no particular skill which Arthur had which the young people did not, so why did they need his help?

16 Strangers On A Train

A man got on a train and sat in a carriage opposite the one other occupant, a woman whom he had never met before. After the train had moved off, the woman, who did not recognize the man, took a pen and sheet of paper from her bag and handed them to him. He wrote something on the paper and gave it back to her. At the next stop the woman left the train and threw away the note. At no time did the man and woman speak to each other, and their meeting was not prearranged. How can these events be explained?

17 Murder Mystery 1

One night a hotel detective was doing his routine round of inspection when he heard a woman's voice from one of the bedrooms crying out: "Don't shoot, for God's sake, Bill, don't shoot me!" He then heard a gun-shot from the room so he broke down the door to see what was going on. A woman lay dead in one corner of the room, shot through the heart. In the middle of the floor was the gun which had been used to shoot her. On the other side of the room stood a fireman, a doctor, and a teacher. The detective had never seen any of the people in the room before. Nevertheless, he went straight up to the fireman and arrested him for the murder. It was in fact the fireman who had committed the murder, but how did the detective know that?

18 Murder Mystery 2

A woman was found gassed in her bedroom. The unlit gas fire was on, and the windows and door were locked from the inside. Her mother had seen her entering the room earlier in the day. It looked like suicide, but in fact the woman had been murdered by her husband.

How did he do it?

19 Murder Mystery 3

A man got into a taxi one afternoon and gave his destination to the driver. No further conversation took place. After a couple of miles, the taxi driver stopped the cab in an isolated spot. He beckoned the man to get out. The driver then picked up a sharp stone, battered his passenger to death, and drove off. The taxi driver had never met the man before and did not know who he was. The driver had no criminal record and he did not rob the passenger.

So why did he kill him?

20 Murder Mystery 4

A man walked into a drugstore and asked for a tube of toothpaste. The man behind the counter pulled out a gun and shot the man. Why would he do that?

21 Murder Mystery 5

A man walked into a pub and asked for a drink. The publican had never seen the man before, but without saying a word he pulled out a gun and shot him dead.

Why would he do that?

22 Kings and Queens

Three playing cards have been removed from an ordinary pack of cards and placed face down in a horizontal row. To the right of a King there are one or two Queens. To the left of a Queen there are one or two Queens. To the left of a Heart there are one or two Spades. To the right of a Spade there are one or two Spades.

What are the three cards?

23 Hijack

A man hijacked a passenger aircraft on an internal flight from Glasgow to London. He ordered the pilot at gunpoint to fly to Birmingham Airport. He used the aircraft's radio to make his demands known to the authorities in Birmingham, namely that he would release the plane and its passengers in return for £100,000 and two parachutes. When the plane landed, he was given the money and the parachutes. The hijacker then demanded that the pilot take off again.

When they were over a sparsely -populated part of the country, he put on one of the parachutes and leapt from the plane with the moneybag. The second parachute was not used, and the hijacker was never found. Why did he ask for two parachutes since he used only one?

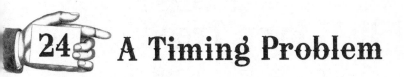

24 A Timing Problem

You have one hourglass which takes 7 minutes for the sand to run out, and one which takes 11 minutes. What is the best way to use these hourglasses to time exactly 15 minutes?

25 The Line and The Rectangle

On a sheet of squared paper, mark out a rectangle one square by two squares in size.

Join a pair of opposite corners with a line, a diagonal. How many squares does it slice through? As you see, two squares. Do the same for a bigger rectangle, two by three squares say. The diagonal cuts four squares.

Can you say how many squares will be cut by the diagonal of a rectangle six by seven squares – without drawing and counting? In short, can you work out a rule? Be careful to work only with rectangles, not squares. It's much harder to find a rule for squares.

26 Even Tread

I keep one spare tyre in my car. Last year I drove 10,000 miles in my car, and rotated the tyres at intervals so that by the end of the year each of the five tyres had been used for the same number of miles. For how many miles was each tyre used?

27 Choose a Glass

Some detectives were investigating a case of poisoning at a hotel. They had lined up a number of partly-filled glasses on a table in the hotel lounge, knowing that only one glass contained poison. They wanted to identify which one before testing it for fingerprints. The problem was that if the police laboratory were asked to test the liquid in each glass, it would take too long. So the inspector in charge contacted a statistician at the local polytechnic to see if there was a quicker way. He came over to the hotel, counted the glasses, smiled, and said:

"Choose any glass, Inspector, and we'll test it first."

The inspector was worried that this would mean the waste of one test, but the statistician denied this.

Later that evening, the inspector was telling his wife about the incident.

"How many glasses were there to start with?" she asked.

"I don't remember exactly – somewhere between 100 and 200 I think," replied the inspector.

Can you work out the exact number of glasses? (Assume that any group of glasses can be tested simultaneously by taking a small sample of liquid from each, mixing the samples and making a single test on the mixture.)

28 21 Bottles of Wine

You have 21 bottles of wine. Seven bottles are full, seven half-full and seven empty. Can you divide the bottles into three equal lots, so that each lot contains the same number of full, half-full and empty bottles? You can only use the bottles but no other measuring instruments.

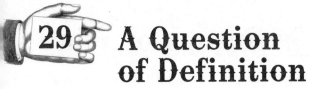

29 A Question of Definition

Two farmers were discussing their holdings. "My property is exactly a mile square," said the first. "Curiously enough, mine is a square mile," replied the second. "Then there is no difference," said the first. Is this correct?

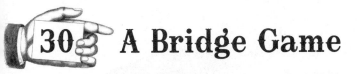

30 A Bridge Game

In a bridge game, all the cards are dealt to four players – 13 cards to each – who usually play as partners, one pair against the other. That should be all you need to know in order to answer these two questions about situations that might arise in a game.

FLUSH. You and your partner have been dealt a surprising hand. Together you have all 13 cards of one suit. Is this event more or less likely than one in which you and your partner together have no cards in one of the suits?

PAPER PERFECT. Every few years a newspaper story will report that players at a local bridge game were witness to a 'perfect deal': that is, each player got all 13 cards of a suit. How many of these deals would you expect to occur anywhere in the world during this decade?

(a) 100+, (b) 50-99, (c) 11-49, (d) 1-10, (e) about 1, (f) about 0.

31 Fruity

You have a bowl of various fruit. All but two of them are apples, all but two of them are bananas and all but two of them are oranges. How many pieces of fruit do you have?

32 The Handicap Race

Mel and Sid race each other in a 100-yard dash. Mel wins by ten yards. They decide to race again, but this time, to make things fairer, Mel begins ten yards behind the starting line. Assuming they both run with the same constant speed as before, who wins this time, Mel or Sid? Or do they tie?

33 The South Pole

Base to explorer at the South Pole: "What's the temperature?"

"Minus 40 degrees" said the explorer.

"Is that Centigrade or Fahrenheit?" asked base.

"Put down Fahrenheit," said the explorer. "I don't expect it will matter."

Why did she say that?

34 The Sequence

Where would you place 9 and 10 to keep the sequence going?

1	2				6	
		3	4	5	7	8

35 Guinness or Stout

Two strangers enter a pub. The publican asks them what they would like. First man says, "I'll have a bottle of stout," and puts 50p down on the counter. Publican: "Guinness at 50p, or Jubilee at 45p?" First man: "Jubilee." Second man says, "I'll have a bottle of stout," and puts 50p on the counter. Without asking him, the publican gives him Guinness. How did he know what he required?

36 A Cup of Tea

Man calls to waiter in the restaurant, "There's a fly in my tea." "I will bring you a fresh cup of tea," says the waiter. After a few moments the man calls out, "This is the same cup of tea!" How did he know?

37 Rope Thief

In a church tower, there are two bell ropes which pass through small holes a foot apart in a high ceiling and hang down to the floor of a room. A circus acrobat, carrying a knife, intends to steal as much of the two ropes as possible. He discovers that the stairs leading above the ceiling are barred by a locked door. Since there are no ladders or other objects on which he can stand, he must carry out the theft by climbing up the ropes hand over hand and cutting them at points as high as possible. The ceiling is so high, however, that a fall from even one-third the height could be fatal. What procedure should he use to obtain a maximum length of rope?

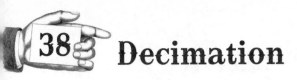

38 Decimation

When the Roman army needed to punish a large number of men, every tenth soldier was executed – hence the word 'decimate'.

You are one of a band of 1,000 mutinous pirates, captured and tied to numbered posts arranged in a circle.

The first is to be executed, then each alternate pirate, until one remains, who will go free.

Which number post would you choose?

39 A Third of The Planet

How far from the earth would you have to be to see one third of the planet's surface?

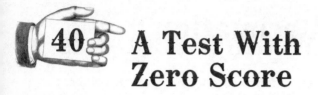

40 A Test With Zero Score

On a 26-question test, five points were deducted for each wrong answer and eight points were credited for each correct answer. If all the questions were answered, how many were correct if the score was zero?

41 Bonus Payments

A company offered its 350 employees a bonus of $10 to each male and $8.15 to each female. All the females accepted, but a certain percentage of the males refused to accept. The total bonus paid was not dependent upon the number of men employed. What was the total amount paid to the women?

42 Weather Analysis

During a period of days, it was observed that when it rained in the afternoon, it had been clear in the morning, and when it rained in the morning, it was clear in the afternoon. It rained on 9 days, and was clear on 6 afternoons and 7 mornings. What is the shortest possible length of this period?

43 A Shuffled Deck

Prove that if the top 26 cards of an ordinary shuffled deck contain more red cards than there are black cards in the bottom 26, then there are in the deck at least three consecutive cards of the same colour.

44 ☞ Antifreeze

A 21-quart capacity car radiator is filled with an 18 percent alcohol solution. How many quarts must be drained and then replaced by a 90 percent alcohol solution for the resulting solution to contain 42 percent alcohol?

45 ☞ A Peculiar Number

If a certain number is reduced by 7 and the remainder is multiplied by 7, the result is the same as when the number is reduced by 11 and the remainder is multiplied by 11. Find the number.

46 Tree Leaves

If there are more trees than there are leaves on any one tree, then there exist at least two trees with the same number of leaves. True or false?

47 The Will

Daniel Greene was killed in a car crash while on his way to the maternity hospital where his wife, Sheila, was about to give birth. He had recently made a new will in which he had stated that should the baby be a boy then his estate was to be divided two-thirds to his son and one third to Sheila; if the baby were a girl then she was to receive one quarter of the estate and Sheila the other three-quarters.

In the event, Sheila gave birth to twins – a boy and a girl. How best should Daniel's estate be divided so as to carry out his intentions?

If a man walks to work and rides back home it takes him an hour and a half. When he rides both ways it takes 30 minutes. How long would it take him to make the round trip by walking?

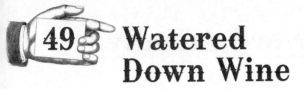

49 Watered Down Wine

Imagine you have two large pitchers. One contains a gallon of water and the other a gallon of wine. One pint of wine is removed from the wine pitcher, poured into the water pitcher and mixed thoroughly. Then a pint of the mixture from the water pitcher is removed and poured into the wine pitcher.

Is there now more or less water in the wine pitcher than there is wine in the water pitcher?

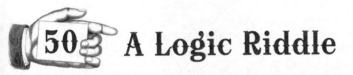

50 A Logic Riddle

In olden days, the student of logic was given this problem:

If half of 5 were 3, what would one-third of 10 be?

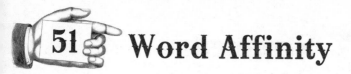

51 Word Affinity

Which word in the bottom row can be logically linked with the words in the top row?

BAG FORCE LINE MAIL TIGHT
RAG HORSE PINE RAID RIGHT

52 Change a Dollar

A man asked a cashier to give him change for a dollar. She looked in her till and then said she was sorry but she couldn't do it with the coins she had. He then asked her for change for half a dollar. Again, she said she couldn't do it, and added that she not could give him change for a quarter, dime or nickel either. When the man asked her if she had any coins at all in her till, she told him she had $1.15 worth. What coins did she have?

53 Streetcars

A man is walking down a street along which runs a streetcar line. He notices that, for every 40 streetcars which pass him travelling in the same direction as him, 60 pass in the opposite direction. If the man's walking speed is 3 mph what is the average speed of the streetcars?

54 A Matter of Health

If 70% of the population have defective eyesight, 75% are hard of hearing, 80% have sinus trouble and 85% suffer from allergies, what percentage (minimum) suffer from all four ailments?

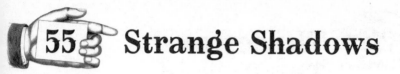

55 Strange Shadows

There is an object which, if a candle is held underneath it, casts a circular shadow on the ceiling. If a candle is held due south of it, a square shadow is cast on the north wall. If a candle is held due east of it, a triangular shadow is cast on the west wall. Can you identify the object?

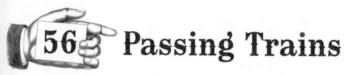

56 Passing Trains

A man and a woman are walking along a railway track. A train passes the man in ten seconds. Twenty minutes later it reaches the woman. It passes her in nine seconds. How long after the train leaves the woman will the man and woman meet if all speeds are constant?

The Fly and The Record

A fly is walking along the groove of a 33 r.p.m. record. The record is lying flat on the floor, and when looked at from above, the fly appears to be travelling clockwise. If it carries on in this way, will it eventually arrive at the edge of the record or the centre?

58  The Hermit

At sunrise on Monday, a hermit began climbing the narrow path to his hut at the top of a mountain. He did not walk at a constant speed but stopped occasionally to eat or rest, reaching his hut shortly before sunset. On Tuesday morning he descended the same path, starting at sunrise and again walking at varying rates, though generally at a faster pace than his average speed going up. Prove that there is a spot along the path that the hermit will occupy on each trip at precisely the same time of day.

59  The Unbalanced Coin

You have a coin that you have reason to suspect is unbalanced – that is, it is biased towards heads or tails, and a long series of tosses won't come out 50-50. How can this coin be used to generate a series of random binary digits – ones and zeros.

60 Bicycle Experiment

A rope is tied to the pedal of a bicycle. If someone pulls back on the rope while another person holds the seat lightly to keep the bicycle balanced, will the bicycle move forward, backward, or not at all?

61 Two Trains

If it takes twice as long for a passenger train to pass a freight train after it first overtakes it as it takes for the two trains to pass each other when going in opposite directions, how many times faster than the freight train is the passenger train?

62 Avoiding The Train

A man was walking down a railway track when he saw an express train speeding toward him. To avoid it he jumped off the track, but before he jumped he ran ten feet toward the train. Why?

63 Boxes and Balls

Four girls were given identical boxes: one containing three black balls, one containing two black balls and one white ball, one containing one black ball and two white balls, and the fourth containing three white balls. Each box had a label on it reading 'Three Black' or 'Two Black, One White' or 'One Black, Two White' or 'Three White'. The girls were told that none of the four labels correctly described the contents of the box to which it was attached. Each girl saw only the label of the box assigned to her. Each one was then asked to close her eyes, remove two balls from her box, and then try to guess the colour of the remaining ball.

The first girl removed two black balls then announced, "I have drawn two black balls, and I know the colour of the third ball." The second girl removed one white and one black ball, and similarly stated, "I have drawn one white and one black ball, and I know the colour of the third ball." The third girl removed two white balls, looked at the label, and said "I have drawn two white balls, but I can't tell what the colour of the third ball is." Finally, the fourth girl, who was blind and therefore could not read the label on her box, declared "I don't need to remove any balls from my box. I know the colour of all three. What's more, I know the colour of the third ball in each of your boxes as well."

The first three girls were amazed by the blind girl's assertion and immediately challenged her. She quickly and logically convinced them that she was entirely correct in saying that she knew the contents of each box. How did she tell?

64 Weather

Bill was checking the weather forecast one night. "Rain for next 48hrs; sunny in 72hrs," it said. "Wrong again," complained Bill. Why?

65 Rhys

In the Kingdom of Powys, a man known as Rhys the Red suffered a strange and terrible fate. He died on October 14th, and was buried two days earlier, on October 12th, of the same year.

How did this come to be?

66 Jasmin's Age

When Jasmin went to the polling station to vote, the clerk asked her age. She told him, 'Eighteen.' He looked at her, surprised, and said 'Are you sure that's right?' Jasmin laughed and replied, 'No, I gave myself the benefit of a year less than a quarter of my real age.' The clerk couldn't calculate how old she actually was, though he did allow her to register her vote. What was Jasmin's age?

67 John and The Chicken

John was attempting to steal a chicken. When he first saw the bird, he was standing 250 yards due south of it. Both began running at the same time and ran with uniform speeds. The chicken ran due east. Instead of running north-east on a straight line, John ran so that at every instant he was running directly towards the chicken.

Assuming that John ran one and one-third times faster than the chicken, how far did the chicken run before he was caught?

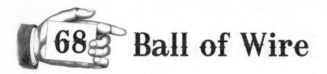

68 Ball of Wire

A wire of one-hundredth of an inch diameter is tightly wound into a ball with a diameter of 24 inches. It is assumed that the wire is bound so solidly that there is no air gap in the ball. What is the length of the wire?

69 Bicycle Rider

A bicycle rider rode one mile in three minutes with the wind, and returned in four minutes against the wind. Assuming that at all times he applies the same force to his pedals, how long would it take him to ride a mile if there were no wind?

70 Counters in Cups

I had doubts whether this puzzle should be included, as it is a borderline case between a trick question and a legitimate puzzle. However, the solution is particularly neat.

How can ten counters be distributed between three cups so that each cup contains an odd number of counters?

71 Ferry Boats

Two ferry boats start moving at the same instant from opposite sides of the Hudson River, one boat going from New York to Jersey City, and the other from Jersey City to New York. One boat is faster than the other, so they meet at a point 720 yards from the nearest shore.

After arriving at their destinations, each boat remains just ten minutes to change passengers before starting on the return trip. The boats meet again at a point 400 yards from the other shore.

What is the exact width of the river?

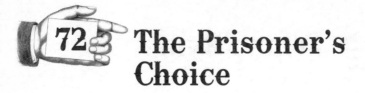

72 The Prisoner's Choice

A prisoner was about to be executed but was promised his freedom if he drew a green ball from one of two similar urns. He was allowed to distribute 50 green and 50 red balls between the two urns any way he liked, then he had to draw one ball at random from one of the urns.

How did the prisoner maximise his chances of success? If he had put equal numbers of green and red balls into one of the urns, the other urn would also contain equal numbers of green and red balls, and thus the probability of his drawing a green one would have been 1/2. Can you improve these chances, and if so, how?

73 Speed of Ant

A tube train is approaching Leicester Square Station at 114 inches per second. A passenger in one carriage is walking forward at 36 inches per second relative to the seat. He is eating a foot-long hot dog, which is entering his mouth at the rate of 2 inches per second. An ant on the hot dog is running away from the man's mouth at 1 inch per second. How fast is the ant approaching Leicester Square Station?

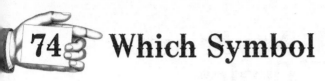

74 Which Symbol

Which familiar mathematical symbol can be placed between 2 and 3 to express a number that is greater than 2 but less than 3?

75 Clock Chimes

You are in a pitch-black room at dead of night, with a clock which chimes the hour, and also once at quarter past, half past and quarter to the hour. If you hear the clock chime once, what is the longest time you may have to wait to be sure what time it is?

76 Word Series

What is the next word in this series: aid, nature, world, estate, column, sense...?

Is it (a) water, (b) music, (c) welcome, or (d) heaven?

77 Wayne and Shirley

Wayne and Shirley have agreed that they would like to have a family of four children, but they would prefer not to have them all the same sex. Is it more likely that they will have three of one sex and one of the other or two of each? (Assume that each birth has an equal chance of being a boy or a girl.)

Shooting Match

Two sharp-shooters, Bill and Ben, had a contest to see which of them was the better shot. In their first session, each fired 50 rounds and hit the target 25 times. Later they had a second session, and this time Bill hit the target 3 times in 34 shots, and Ben missed 25 shots in a row before giving up. Since Bill's record in the second session was better than Ben's, Bill argued that his record for the two sessions combined was better than Ben's. Was he right?

Gun Problem

I have a gun I use for clay-pigeon shooting. This gun is 1.7 yards long. One day I wanted to take the train to join a shooting party, but the ticket clerk told me that it was against the regulations for a passenger to take a firearm into the carriage, and it couldn't be put in the baggage area either because the baggage handler wasn't allowed to take any article whose greatest dimension exceeded 1 yard. What did I do to ensure that both I and my gun were allowed on the train?

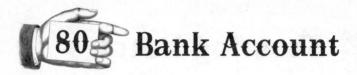

Bank Account

A bank customer had £100 in his account. He then made six withdrawals, totalling £100. He kept a record of these withdrawals, and the balance remaining in the account as follows:

Withdrawals	Balance left
£50	£50
£25	£25
£10	£15
£8	£7
£5	£2
£2	0
——	——
£100	£99

When he added up the columns as above, he assumed that he must owe £1 to the bank. Was he right?

81 Toss The Pennies

Jill offered Jack the following bet: she said she would toss three coins in the air, and if they fell all heads or all tails she would give him £1. If they fell any other way, he had to give her 50p.

Should Jack accept the bet?

82 Counter Colours

A bag contains one counter, which may be either black or white. A second counter, which is definitely white, is put into the bag. The bag is shaken and one counter taken out, which proves to be white. What is the probability of the next counter coming out of the bag also being white?

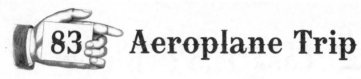

83 Aeroplane Trip

An aeroplane flies from London to Paris, then back again. When there is no wind, its average ground speed, ie speed relative to the ground, for the entire trip is 100 miles per hour. Assume that a steady wind is blowing in a straight direction from London towards Paris. How will this affect the plane's average ground speed for the round trip, assuming that it flies at all times with the same motor speed as before?

The temptation is to say that it won't affect the average speed at all because it will speed up the plane on its flight to Paris and slow it down on its return to London by the same amount. However, by this reasoning, if the wind speed were 100 miles an hour, the plane would go from London to Paris at 200 miles an hour but it wouldn't be able to get back to London because its return speed would be zero. Is that right?

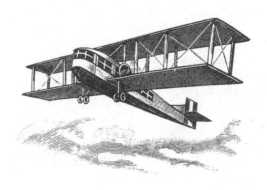

84 Traffic Lights

The High Street in our town has a linked traffic system consisting of six consecutive sections, each a multiple of one-eighth of a mile in length, and each terminating in a traffic light. These traffic lights are synchronized so that a vehicle travelling at 30 mph will pass each light at the same point in its 26-second operating cycle. This cycle can be considered as 13 seconds on red (stop) and 13 seconds on green (go).

My brother, Albert, had studied the system and reckoned that he could drive faster than 30 mph and still get through the whole system without crossing a red light. He set up an experiment with the collaboration of his friends Hubert and Robert. All three of them entered the first section simultaneously, Albert travelling at 30 mph, Hubert at 50 mph, and Robert at 75 mph, with the first traffic light turning green three seconds later.

Robert got through the whole system in less than two minutes without being stopped. However, he thought that he had just been lucky, as he arrived at the last light just as it changed to red. Hubert ran out of petrol after the third light, and in any case would have been stopped at the second light had he not lost ten seconds due to a delay in the second section.

What were the lengths of each of the six sections?

85 A Boy, A Girl and A Dog

A boy, a girl and a dog start at the same spot on a straight road. The boy walks forward at four miles per hour; the girl walks forward at three miles per hour. Meanwhile, the dog trots back and forth between them at 10 miles per hour. Assuming that each reversal of direction of the dog is instantaneous, where is it and which way is it facing after one hour?

Hat in The River

A man wearing a straw hat was fishing from a rowing boat in a river that flowed at a speed of 3 miles an hour. The boat drifted down the river at the same rate.

Just as the man started to row upstream, the wind blew his hat off his head and into the water beside the boat. However, he didn't notice that his hat was gone until he had rowed 5 miles upstream, at which point he immediately started rowing back downstream to retrieve his hat.

The man's rowing speed in still water is a constant 5 miles an hour. However, when rowing upstream his speed relative to the shore would be only 2 miles an hour, given the rate of flow of the river. Rowing downstream, his speed relative to the shore would be 8 miles an hour for the same reason.

If the man lost his hat at 2 o'clock in the afternoon, what was the time when he retrieved it?

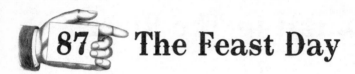

87 The Feast Day

In a remote village high in the Himalayas a Feast Day is declared whenever the bells of the temple and the monastery ring at exactly the same time. The temple bell rings at regular intervals of a whole number of minutes. Similarly the monastery bell rings at regular intervals but of a different whole number of minutes. Today the bells are due to ring together at 12 noon.

Between Feast Days, the bells of the temple and monastery ring alternately, and although they only coincide on Feast Days they do occur as little as a minute apart on some other days.

The last time the bells coincided was at 12 noon a prime number of days ago. How many days ago was that?

88 The Kings

Six playing cards are lying face-down on the table. Two, and only two, of them are kings, but you don't know which. You pick two cards at random and turn them face-up. Which is more likely:

a) that there will be at least one king among the two cards, or

b) that there will be no king among the two cards?

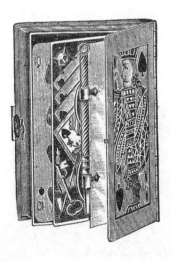

89 The Clock-mender

I have two clocks which, when fully wound, will run for nearly eight days before stopping. Both of these clocks were keeping different times, and each was wrong by an exact number of minutes per day, though less than one hour in each case.

I took my clocks to our local clock-mender, who works 9.30 am to 5.00 pm, Mondays to Fridays. He immediately wound both clocks fully and set them to the right time – a whole number of minutes after the hour – and put them on a shelf for observation.

The following Monday, as he went to take down the clocks to start work on them, they both started to strike 8 o'clock simultaneously. This was some hours and minutes pass the correct time. What day and exact time was it when he originally set them?

90 Red White Blue

This is a famous paradox which has caused a great deal of argument and disbelief from many who cannot accept the correct answer.

Four balls are placed in a hat. One is white, one is blue and the other two are red. The bag is shaken and someone draws two balls from the hat. He looks at the two balls and announces that at least one of them is red. What are the chances that the other ball he has drawn out is also red?

91 Qualifications

One hundred job-seekers applied for a technical position. Of these, ten had never taken a course in engineering or computer science, 75 had taken at least one course in engineering, and 83 had taken at least one course in computer science. How many of the applicants had done some studies in both engineering and computer science?

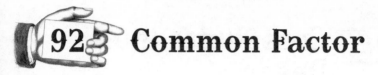

92 Common Factor

What do the following words have in common?

**DEFT FIRST CALMNESS CANOPY LAUGHING
STUPID HIJACK**

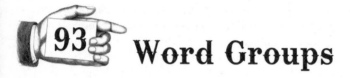

93 Word Groups

Which word from Group 2 belongs with those in Group 1?

Group 1: **BAG STORM BANK BAR**
Group 2: **MOON FLOOR STORE DUNE**

94 The Commuter

Henry lives in a suburb and commutes to the city by train. He either walks to the station and his wife picks him up by car on his return, or she takes him to the station in the morning and he walks home in the evening. Either way, the round trip takes one hour. If Henry were to take the car both ways it would take 20 minutes. How long would a round trip take if he walked both ways?

95 Crossing The Desert

A small aeroplane carrying three men has to make an emergency landing in the middle of the desert. The men decide that their best chance for survival is for each of them to set out across the desert in a different direction, in the hope that one of the three will be able to reach civilization and get help for the others. Their supplies include five full bottles of water, five half-full, and five empty bottles. Since water-carrying capacity is important should a man reach an oasis, they wish to divide both the water supply and the number of bottles equally among themselves. How can they achieve this?

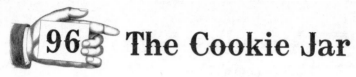

96 The Cookie Jar

An old nursery rhyme starts:

'Who stole the cookie from the cookie jar...'

Let us find out from the following statements, of which only one is true:

Ann: Harry stole the cookie from the cookie jar.
Harry: Fred stole the cookie from the cookie jar.
Lisa: Who, me? Can't be.
Fred: Harry is lying when he says that I stole the cookie.

97 A Deck of Cards

Imagine shuffling a deck of cards, then dealing them face-up, one at a time. As you deal, you recite aloud the names of all the cards in the deck in a predetermined order, for example ace through to the king of spades, then the same for hearts, diamonds and clubs. Now, is it sensible for you to offer an even-money bet that at least one card you turn up will be the same as the card you name out loud?

98 Two Wins

Bill is a keen chess-player, and plays often against his parents. He wins and loses against both parents, but his father is a better player than his mother.

His father offers to double Bill's pocket money if he can win two games in a row out of three, with his parents alternating as opponents. Which parent should Bill play first to maximize his chances of winning two games in succession?

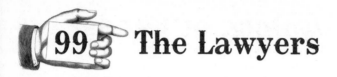

99 The Lawyers

Eugene P. Northrop, in his book *Riddles in Mathematics*, poses this problem:

A paradox which has its foundation – real or legendary – in antiquity concerns the sophist Protagoras, who lived and taught in the fifth century BC. It is said that Protagoras made an agreement with one of his pupils whereby the pupil was to pay for his legal instruction after he had won his first case. The young man completed his course, hung up the traditional sign, and waited for clients. None appeared. Protagoras grew impatient and decided to sue his former pupil for the amount owed him.

"For," argued Protagoras, "either I win this suit, or you win it. If I win, you pay me according to the judgement of the court. If you win, you pay me according to our agreement. In either case I am bound to be paid."

"Not so," replied the young man. "If I win, then by the judgement of the court I need not pay you. If you win, then by our agreement I need not pay you. In either case I am bound not to have to pay you."

Whose argument was right? Who knows?

I do not agree that the answer is as inconclusive as indicated. What is your opinion: will the pupil have to pay?

100 Find X

Solve the following equation for X:

$$\sqrt{X + \sqrt{X + \sqrt{X...}}} = 2$$

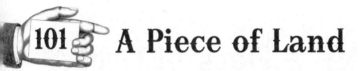

101 A Piece of Land

Jason wants a piece of land, exactly level, with four boundary lines. Two of the boundary lines must run exactly north-south and the other two exactly east-west. Each boundary line must measure exactly 100 feet. Can Jason buy such a piece of land in England?

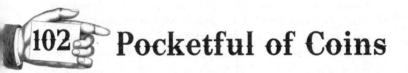

102 Pocketful of Coins

Freddy has 10 pockets and 44 pound coins. He wants to distribute his pounds in his pockets so that each pocket contains a different number of coins. Can he do this?

103 Gallons

How can you remove exactly six gallons of water from a tank using just two containers – a nine-gallon bucket and a four-gallon bucket?

104 A Flock of Geese

Two brothers, Guy and George, inherited a flock of geese. They sold all of them, receiving for each goose the same number of pounds as there were geese in the flock. The money was given to them in £10 notes except for an excess amount, less than £10, that was in pound coins. They divided the notes between them by placing them on a table and alternately taking a note until there were none left. Guy complained that this was not fair because George took both the first and last notes and thus got £10 more. To even things up somewhat, George gave Guy all the pound coins, but Guy argued that he was still owed some money. George agreed to give Guy a cheque to make the total amounts equal. What was the value of the cheque?

Three Points on A Hemisphere

Three points are selected at random on a sphere's surface. What is the probability that all three lie on the same hemisphere? Assume that the great circle, bordering a hemisphere, is part of the hemisphere.

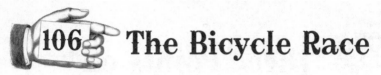

106 The Bicycle Race

Two cyclists are racing around a circular track. Pierre can ride once around the track in six minutes, and Louis in four minutes. How many minutes will it take for Louis to overtake Pierre?

107 Check The Equations

Four of the following equations are wrong. Correct them.

(a) $2 + 2 = 4$

(b) $4 \div \frac{1}{2} = 2$

(c) $3\frac{1}{5} \times 3\frac{1}{8} = 10$

(d) $7 - (-4) = 11$

(e) $-10(6 - 6) = -10$

(f) $1 \div 0 = 0$

(g) $1 \div \infty = \infty$ (∞ is the symbol for infinity)

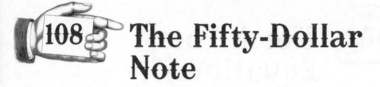

108 The Fifty-Dollar Note

A banker picked up a $50 note which was lying in the gutter, and made a note of its number. When he arrived home, his wife told him that she had received a bill from the butcher for $50. He gave her the note and she paid the butcher. The butcher paid it to a farmer from whom he bought a calf, and the farmer paid it to a merchant who in turn paid it to a laundry-woman. The laundry-woman used it to pay off her $50 overdraft at the bank. The banker recognized the note as the one he had found. By that time it had paid off $250 worth of debts. On examination, however, he discovered that it was counterfeit. What was lost in the whole transaction, and by whom?

109 Multiplication

How quickly can you calculate the following?

1 x 2 x 3 x 4 x 5 x 6 x 7 x 8 x 9 x 0

110 North Pole

A man goes to the North Pole. The points of the compass are, of course:

N

W   E

S

He reaches the Pole and, having passed over it, turns about to look North. East is now on his left-hand side, and West on his right-hand side, so the points of the compass would appear to be:

N

E   W

S

What is the explanation?

111 Cross The Desert

A desert 800 miles wide has an unlimited supply of petrol available at one edge but no source within the desert itself. A lorry-load of petrol is enough to go 500 miles, and the driver can build up his own refuelling stations at any point along the way. These stores may be of any size, and assume no evaporation loss. What is the minimum number of lorry-loads of petrol required to cross the desert? And what is the maximum width of desert a lorry can cross in this way?

112 Return The Bottle

A bottle of mineral water costs 25p. The water cost 15p more than the bottle. How much should you receive on returning the bottle?

113 Card Games

Jack and Jill are playing cards for a stake of £1 a game. At the end, Jack has won three games and Jill has won £3. How many games did they play?

114 Long Playing Record

The diameter of a long-playing record is 12 inches. The unused part in the centre has a diameter of 4 inches, and there is a smooth outer edge one inch wide around the recording. If there are 91 grooves to the inch, how far does the needle move during the actual playing of the recording?

115 Cash Bags

A man went into a bank with exactly £1,000, all in £1 coins. He gave the money to a cashier and asked her to put the money into ten bags in such a way that if he asked later for any number of pounds up to £1,000 she could give the exact amount to him in one or more bags without needing to open any of the bags. How was the cashier able to carry out this instruction?

116 Garage Space

A haulage contractor did not have room in his garage for eight of his lorries. He therefore increased the size of his garage by 50 percent, which gave him room for eight more lorries than the number he owned. How many lorries did he own?

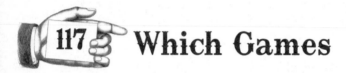

117 Which Games

I have three sporting friends. Two play cricket, two play football and two play rugby. The one who does not play rugby does not play football, and the one who does not play football does not play cricket. Which games does each friend play?

118 What day is it?

When the day after tomorrow is yesterday, today will be as far from Sunday as today was from Sunday when the day before yesterday is tomorrow. What day is it today?

119 Bag of Sweets

Three girls agreed to share out a bag of sweets in proportion to their ages. The sum of their ages was 17½ years, and the bag contained 770 sweets. For every four sweets Joan took, Jane took three, and for every six that Joan took, Jill took seven. How many sweets did each girl take, and what are their respective ages?

120 Lost

I am travelling in a strange country. I have no map. I come to a crossroads where a signpost has been knocked down. How can I find my way without asking anyone for directions?

Problem Age

The day before yesterday Peter was 17. Next year he will be 20. How do you explain this?

Panama Canal

A ship entered the Panama Canal at its west end, passed through the canal, and left it at its east end. However, immediately it left the canal it entered the Pacific Ocean. If the ship did not double back nor sail backwards, how could this be so?

The Shortcut

John was trying to take a shortcut through a very narrow tunnel when he heard the whistle of an approaching train behind him. Having reached three-eights of the length of the tunnel, he could have turned back and cleared the entrance of the tunnel running at 10 mph. just as the train entered. Alternatively, if he kept running forward, the train would reach him the moment he would jump clear of the tracks. At what speed was the train travelling?

124 How Many Coins

My mother told me that the coins she had in her purse enabled her to pay the exact price for any item from one cent up to and including one dollar, without receiving any change. What is the smallest number of coins she could have had in her purse?

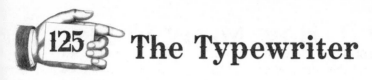

125 The Typewriter

My typewriter used to have a standard keyboard, with the letters arranged as follows:

Row 1 **Q W E R T Y U I O P**
Row 2 **A S D F G H J K L**
Row 3 **Z X C V B N M**

I lent the machine to a friend, and when it came back I found that the positions of the letters had been altered into what he claimed was a more efficient layout. None of the letters was in its original row, though the numbers of letters in each row remained unchanged.

I tested the new layout by typing various words connected with my business – I run an off-licence. The numbers in brackets below show the number of rows I had to use to produce each word:

BEER (1)
STOUT (1)
SHERRY (2)
WHISKY (3)
HOCK(2)
LAGER (2)
VODKA (2)
CAMPARI (2)
CIDER (3)
SQUASH (2, but would have been 1 but for a single letter**)**
FLAGON (2)
MUZZY (2)

The next word I tried was **CHAMBERTIN**. Which rows, in order, did I use?

SOLUTIONS

1 Crafty Cabby

The lady realized that the cabby could not be deaf because he drove her to her requested destination.

2 Insomnia

John snored.

3 How Did He Die

The man had tied a noose around his neck and stood on a block of ice. He committee suicide as the ice melted and created the puddle.

4 The Burglars

John is one year old.

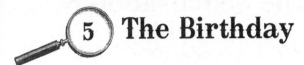

5 The Birthday

Alice had a wealthy boyfriend who wanted to buy her an expensive birthday present. They selected the £4,000 bracelet. As this would have been difficult to explain to her husband, they conspired with the jeweller to go along with the deception.

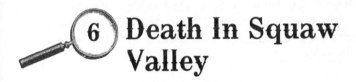

6 Death In Squaw Valley

The clerk remembered having issued the flight tickets to the banker, who had booked return for himself and one way for his wife.

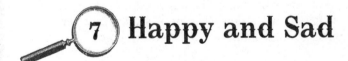

7 Happy and Sad

This is the final of the Miss World Beauty Contest. As everyone knows, the ecstatic winner always cries. The other two woman are smiling because they, the runners-up, are expected to look happy.

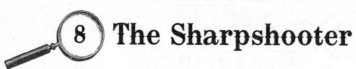

8 The Sharpshooter

The sharpshooter's hat was hung over the end of his gun.

9 The Golfers

Sidney and Stanley were golfers but on this occasion they were playing a game of tennis. The score was 30-all when Stanley hit a shot out. Sidney's subsequent good shot gave him the game.

10 Rash Impulse

The man was the window cleaner. He was standing on the outside ledge of the window when he was stung by a bee. His impulse prompted him to leap *into* the building.

11 Staying Dry

Four of the brothers were carrying the fifth, who stayed dry because he was in his coffin.

12 The Kiss

The young woman gave the stranger mouth-to-mouth resuscitation, the 'kiss of life'.

13 Mass Murder?

The man was a lighthouse keeper, and his lighthouse was built to warn sailors to keep away from a dangerous reef. When the man left and turned off the lights, there was no longer any warning to shipping. A shipwreck occurred, and 142 lives were lost.

14 Communication Problem

The daughters had been separated since birth and didn't speak even a word of each others' languages.

15 Being Neighbourly

Arthur helped the young couple by witnessing their signatures on their wills.

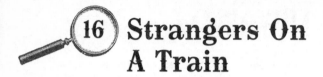

16 Strangers On A Train

The man was an actor who occasionally got bit-parts on television. The woman was a deaf mute. Since the man was chewing gum, the woman thought he might be speaking to her, so she handed him the pen and paper. He assumed that she had recognized him and wanted his autograph, so he signed the paper. This meant nothing to her, so she threw it away when she got off the train.

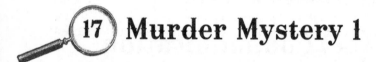

17 Murder Mystery 1

The doctor and the teacher were women, so the fireman was the only person in the room whose name could have been Bill.

18 Murder Mystery 2

The woman had lit the gas fire in the bedroom before she had fallen asleep. Then her husband turned off the main gas supply to the house, causing the fire to go out. When he turned it on again gas from the unlit fire filled the bedroom and asphyxiated the woman.

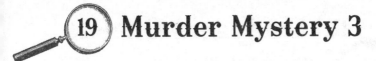

19 Murder Mystery 3

The destination the man gave to the taxi-driver was the driver's own home address. The driver knew that his wife had a lover who visited her in the afternoons. He therefore murdered the man believing him to be his wife's lover.

20 Murder Mystery 4

The man behind the counter was in the process of robbing the drugstore. He had already shot the proprietor and now he shot the customer in order to eliminate him as a witness to the crime.

21 Murder Mystery 5

The wife of the publican had been killed by the identical twin of the man who came in for a drink. The murderer had been acquitted in court on a technicality. The publican had been in court and, not knowing about the twin, assumed that the man in the shop was the murderer and shot him in revenge.

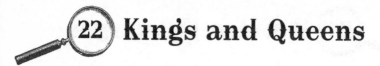

22 Kings and Queens

There are only two arrangements of Kings and Queens which can satisfy the first and second statements, these being KQQ and QKQ. The third and fourth statements are met by only two possible arrangements of Hearts and Spades, these being SSH and SHS. These two sets can be combined in four possible ways as follows:

KS, QS, QH
KS, QH, QS
QS, KS, QH
QS, KH, QS

The final set is ruled out because it contains two Queens of Spades. Since all the other sets consists of the King of Spades, Queen of Spades and Queen of Hearts, these must be the three cards on the table. It is not possible to state definitely which position any particular card is in, but the first must be a Spade and the third a Queen.

23 Hijack

The hijacker asked for two parachutes in order to trick the authorities into believing that he intended to take a hostage. If he had asked for only one, they would have known it was for him and might have supplied a dud. By asking for two, he ensured that two good parachutes would be supplied, one of which he could use for his escape.

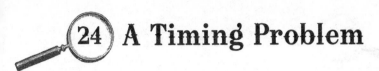

24 A Timing Problem

The 'best' solution depends on whether you want the quickest method or the simplest. Both are given here.

The quickest method is to start by turning over both the 7-minute and the 11-minute hourglasses. As soon as the sand has stopped running in the 7-minute hourglass, turn it over again. As soon as the sand has stopped in the 11-minute hourglass, turn the 7-glass again. When the sand has stopped running in the 7-minute hourglass, the 15 minutes will have elapsed.

This solution takes longer – 22 minutes in total – but is simpler in that it requires only one turn of an hourglass. As before, start by turning over both the 7-minute and the 11-minute hourglasses. The point at which the sand has stopped running in the 7-minute hourglass is the start of the 15 minute timing. When the 11-minute hourglass has run out, turn it over. When it has run out a second time, then 15 minutes will have elapsed.

25 The Line and The Rectangle

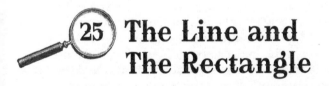

In a six-by-seven rectangle, the diagonal cuts 12 squares. Rule: add the length to the width and subtract 1.

26 Even Tread

Each tyre was used for four-fifths of the total mileage: four-fifths of 10,000 miles = 8,000 miles per tyre.

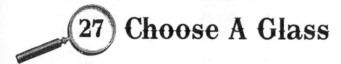

27 Choose A Glass

The binary procedure is the most efficient method for testing any number of glasses of liquid in order to identify a single glass containing poison. First the glasses are divided as nearly in half as possible. Then one set is tested by taking a sample from each glass, combining them, and testing the mixture. The set identified as including the poisoned glass is then divided again as nearly in half as possible, and the procedure repeated until the poisoned glass is identified. If the number of glasses is between 100 and 128 inclusive, as many as seven tests might be required. From 129 to 200 glasses might take eight tests. The number 128 is the turning point. Since we know that the number was between 100 and 200, there must therefore have been 129 glasses in the hotel lounge, because only in that case would the initial testing of one glass make no difference in applying the most efficient testing procedure. To test 129 glasses by halving could result in eight tests. If a single glass were tested first, the remaining 128 glasses would require no more than seven tests, so that the total number of tests remains the same.

When the above answer was first published, many people wrote to say that the detective inspector was right, and the statistician wrong. Regardless of the number of glasses, the most efficient testing procedure is to divide them as nearly in half as possible at each step and test the glasses in either set. When the probabilities are worked out, the expected number of tests of 129 glasses, if the halving procedure is followed, is 7.0155+. But if a single glass is tested first, the expected number is 7.9457+. This is an increase of 0.930+ test, so the inspector was almost right in considering the statistician to be wasteing one test. Only if there had been 129 glasses, however, do we have a plausible excuse for the error, so, in a way, the problem was correctly answered even by those readers who proved that the statistician's test procedure was inefficient.

 28 21 Bottles of Wine

Pour four of the half-full bottles together, to give you nine full, three half-full and nine empty bottles.

 29 A Question of Definition

There is no difference in area between a mile square and a square mile. But there may be considerable difference in the shape. A mile square can only be in the shape of a square. A square mile can be of any shape.

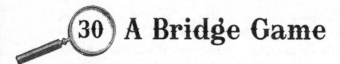

30 A Bridge Game

FLUSH. The two events are equally likely. You may prove this by doing pages of calculations or by using shortcut reasoning. If two players hold all the cards in one suit, the other two players are necessarily void in that suit – the two events occur together, hence they are equally probable.

PAPER PERFECT. All stories of perfect deals in bridge should be taken with a grain of salt. The odds against one are: 2,235,197,406,985,633,368,301,599,999 to 1. This is so remote that a perfect deal has probably never occurred by chance (as opposed to a prank or a poorly shuffled deck) in the entire history of the game. If everyone in the world were dealt 60 bridge hands a day, a perfect deal would occur only once in 124 trillion years.

31 Fruity

Three pieces of fruit.

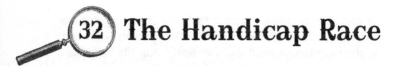

32 The Handicap Race

Mel wins again. In the second race, after Sid has gone 90 yards, Mel will have gone 100, and they will be alongside each other. There are 10 more yards to run, and since Mel is the faster runner, he will finish first.

33 The South Pole

-40 degrees Centigrade = -40 degrees Fahrenheit.

34 The Sequence

9 below, 10 above. Numbers appearing above the line are spelt with three letters only.

35 Guinness or Stout

He puts down 4 x 10p and 2 x 5p coins. If he had required Jubilee he would have put down 4 x 10p and 1 x 5p coins.

36 A Cup of Tea

He had already sugared the tea. When the waiter returned with the supposedly fresh cup, he sugared it again and knew it was the original tea as soon he took the first sip.

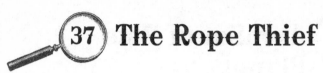

37 The Rope Thief

The acrobat starts by tying together the lower ends of the two ropes. He then climbs rope 1 to the top and cuts rope 2, leaving enough rope to tie into a loop. Hanging in this loop with one arm through it, he cuts rope 1 off at the ceiling, taking great care not to let it fall. He then passes the end of rope 1 through the loop and pulls it until the middle of the tied-together ropes is at the loop. He lets himself down this double rope and then pulls it free of the loop. This enables him to obtain the entire length of rope 1 and almost all of rope 2.

Alternative solutions for this problem have been suggested, some involving knots that could be shaken loose from the ground, others cutting a rope partway through so that it would just support the thief's weight and later could be snapped by a sudden pull. It has also been pointed out that the thief would probably not have got away with any rope at all because his activities would have started the bells ringing.

38 Decimation

976. Take 2 to the power which gives the lowest number above 1000, which is $2^{10} = 1024$.

$$\text{Formula} = 1024 - [(1024 - 1000) \times 2] = 976$$

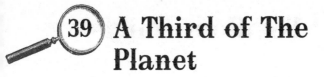

39 A Third of The Planet

You would have to be at a distance equal to the earth's diameter – about 7,900 miles.

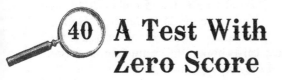

40 A Test With Zero Score

Eight wrong questions cancel out five correct ones, so getting five right out of thirteen –and thus 10 correct out of 26 –will produce a zero score.

41 Bonus Payments

Let m be the number of men and let x be the fraction of men refusing a bonus. Then the amount paid out is given by

$$T = 8.15(350 - m) + 10(1 - x)m = 2852.50 + m(1.85 - 10x)$$

which will be independent of m only if x = 0.185, so that T = 2852.50. Both m and 0.185m are integers with m < 350, so m = 200. It follows that \$1,222.50 is paid to the 150 women.

42 Weather Analysis

You want to stack up as many possible clear days and still have nine rainy days. 2 clear days reduces 6+7 periods to 4+5 (for the rain), giving 9 + 2 or 11 days in the period.

43 A Shuffled Deck

The number of red cards in the top 26 must always equal the number of black cards in the bottom 26. The "If" condition can never be met. Hence by the rules of logic, the statement is correct no matter what follows the word 'then', because it never needs to be considered.

44 Antifreeze

One quart of the old solution differs from one quart of the new (or average) solution by -24 percent, while one quart of the solution to be added differs from the new solution by +48 percent. Hence, there must be two quarts of the old solution for each quart of the added solution. So $1/3$ of the original radiator content or 7 quarts must be drained.

45 A Peculiar Number

The common result must have 7 and 11 as factors, thus the number is 7 + 11 or 18. The method is general, since the solution of $(x - k)k = (x - m)m$ is $k + m$.

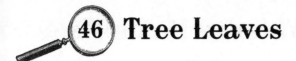

46 Tree Leaves

Yes, with the proviso that if there is just one more tree than the maximum number of leaves, and another tree is leafless, then it might not necessarily be so.

47 The Will

Daniel Greene's evident intention was that his estate be divided 2:1 between his son and his widow, or 1:3 between his daughter and his widow. These ratios can be preserved by giving the son six-tenths of the estate, the daughter one-tenth and his widow, Sheila, three-tenths.

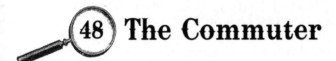

48 The Commuter

Two round trips made the first way would take 3 hours, thus covering the distance between home and office twice walking and twice riding. Therefore, he could make the round trip by walking in 3 - ½ or 2½ hours.

49 Watered Down Wine

There is exactly as much water in the wine pitcher as there is wine in the water pitcher. Regardless of the proportions of wine and water which have been transferred, if both pitchers originally held equal volumes of unadulterated liquids and both are eventually left with equal volumes of mixtures, then equal amounts of wine and water must have been transferred.

This old brain-teaser also forms the basis of a perplexing card trick:

The performer and the spectator are seated opposite each other at a table. The performer turns 20 cards face-up from a pack of 52 cards. The spectator is asked to shuffle the pack so that the reversed cards are randomly distributed, then to hold the pack out of sight beneath the table and to count off 20 cards from the top. These 20 cards are passed, under the table, to the performer.

Having taken the 20 cards, the performer continues to hold them beneath the table, and tells the spectator:

"Neither of us knows how many reversed cards there are in this pack of 20. However, it is likely that there are fewer reversed cards in the pack of 20 than there are in the pack of 32 which you are holding. Without looking at my cards, I am going to turn some more face-down cards face-up in an attempt to equalise the number of reversed cards in my packet with the number in yours."

The performer then fiddles with his packet of cards under the table, making out that he can feel the difference between fronts and backs. After a few moments, he brings them into view and spreads them on the table. When the face-up cards are counted, it turns out that their number is exactly the same as the number of face-up cards in the spectator's packet of 32!

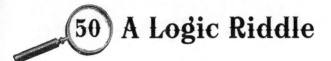

50 A Logic Riddle

The answer is 4. The problem can be written as follows:

$$\frac{5}{2}:3=\frac{10}{3}:x$$

The factor which causes 1/2 x 5 to give the answer 3 must also be introduced into the product 1/3 x 10. This factor is expressed by the ratio 5/2 : 3.

An alternative reasoning goes as follows:

If 2½ = 3, then 10 = 12
.×. 1/3 of 10 = 4

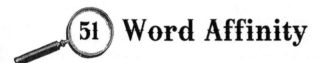

51 Word Affinity

The word RAID can be most easily associated with the top row, as all these words can be preceded by 'AIR'.

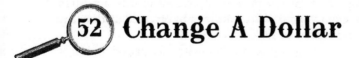

52 Change A Dollar

Since the cashier couldn't change a dollar, the till could not have contained more than one half dollar. Since she couldn't change a half dollar, the till had no more than one quarter and no more than four dimes. Since she couldn't change a dime, the till had no more than one nickel. Since she couldn't change a nickel, the till had no more than four pennies. To summarise:

1 half dollar	$0.50
1 quarter	$0.25
4 dimes	$0.40
1 nickel	$0.05
4 pennies	$0.04
	$1.24

The above would of course provide change for a dollar, and we know that the total was $0.09 less than $1.24. If the nickel and 4 pennies are removed, the remaining coins will not provide change for a dollar and will add up to $1.15. So the answer is a half dollar, a quarter and four dimes.

(53) Streetcars

The solution normally given to this problem uses the method of relative speeds: the relative velocity between man and streetcar when going in the same and opposite directions respectively is proportional to the number of cars encountered. However, a simpler explanation that short-circuits the algebra is this:

$$(x + 3)/(x - 3) = 60/40$$

$$\therefore x = 15 \text{ m.p.h.}$$

Picture two cars at the start of the walk, the 40th car behind the man and the 60th car ahead of him. These must obviously have each travelled half the distance between them when they met at the man, namely, a 50-car space.

So the distance walked in the same period was a 10-car space, or one-fifth as much, which means the speed of the streetcar was 15 mph.

54 A Matter of Health

If there were just two ailments with the percentages 70% and 75%, then the minimum overlap would be 45%, or 70% plus 75% minus 100. The minimum 45% of the population with the first two conditions similarly overlaps the 80% with the third ailment by a minimum of 25%. Finally the minimum of 25% suffering from the first three ailments overlaps the 85% with the fourth condition by at least 10%. The same principle would apply to any other combination of any number of ailments. The answer can be calculated instantly with the following formula:

$$(A1\% + A2\% + A3\% + ... An\%) - 100 \times (N - 1)$$

where A1 ... An are the percentages of the various ailments and N is the number of different ailments.

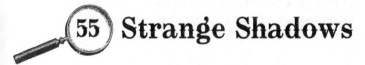

55 Strange Shadows

The object is a disposable paper container, such as are used as drinking cups in American railway cars.

The cups are folded flat for packing purposes. To use one, it has to be opened out making the top circular and the side creases parallel.

56 Passing Trains

If it takes 10 seconds for a train of length L to pass A, and 9 seconds to pass B, the relative velocity between train and A is L/10, between train and B is L/9, and between A and B is L/90. The latter figure is one-tenth the relative velocity between train and B. Since it took the train 1,210 seconds to reach B, it will take A ten times as long, or 12,100 seconds, of which 1,219 seconds had elapsed when the train passed B, leaving 3 hours, 1 minute and 21 seconds.

An alternative, and perhaps more interesting solution, considers an observer looking out of a supposedly stationary train at the two walkers. It appears to such an observer that the woman moves faster than the man, since the woman takes 9 seconds to cover a distance that the man covers in 10 seconds, and thus in a 9 second period the woman gains one second over the man. It is given that the woman goes past the rear end of the train 20 minutes and 9 seconds after the man, and for them to meet it would take 9 times this interval, or 3 hours, 1 minute and 21 seconds.

57 The Fly and The Record

It will arrive at the outer edge. When a record is played on a turntable, it revolves clockwise when seen from above, and relative to the record, the needle moves anticlockwise as seen from above. If the needle – and hence the fly – were to move clockwise around the groove, it would end up at the outer edge.

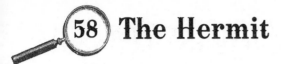

58 The Hermit

Imagine two hermits walking on the same day, one up and one down, both following precisely the path that the real hermit had taken and both proceeding at the same rate of speed as the real hermit. The two imaginary hermits must meet somewhere along the path (though we can't say precisely where), and that is the spot the hermit had occupied on both trips at exactly the same time of day.

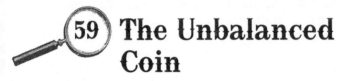

59 The Unbalanced Coin

An unbalanced coin *can* be used to generate a series of truly random numbers. In trying to determine each number, toss the coin twice. Since the coin is biased, the outcome heads-heads (HH) will not occur with the same frequency as tails-tails (TT). But the sequence HT is as likely as TH, no matter how unfair the coin may be. You simply flip the coin twice for each trial, rejecting both HH and TT, then designate HT as 'one' and TH as 'zero' (or vice versa).

60 Bicycle Experiment

Strange as it may seem, pulling back on the lower pedal causes the bicycle to move *backward*. The force on the pedal is in the direction that would normally propel the bicycle forward, but the large size of the wheels and the small gear ratio between the pedal and the wheel sprockets are such that the bicycle is free to move backward with the pull. When it does so, the pedal actually moves forward with respect to the bicycle (that is, in an anti-clockwise direction in the illustration), although it moves backward with respect to the ground.

61 Two Trains

The passenger train is three times as fast as the freight train.

62 Avoiding The Train

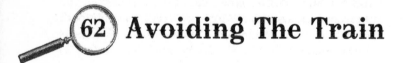

The man was walking in a tunnel.

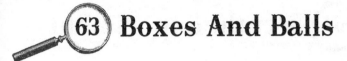

The only combination of boxes and contents for which the first two girls could easily infer the colour of their third ball while the third girl could not, is as follows:

Box	1	2	3	4
Label	BBW	BWW	BBB	WWW
Contents	BBB	BBW	WWW	BWW

The blind girl, referring to the other three as A, B and C respectively, reasoned as follows:

1) If C, having drawn WW cannot tell the colour of the third ball, the label must be marked BBB.
2) If A, having drawn BB, knows the colour of the third ball, then the label must be marked BBW or BBB. However, as BBB is already identified as belonging to C, A's label must be BBW.
3) B, having drawn WB and knowing the colour of the remaining ball, could have labels marked BWW or BBW. However, BBW is eliminated by (2), therefore her label is marked BWW.
4) Finally, the only combination remaining for the blind girl is a label marked WWW, with contents of BWW.

64 Weather

In 72hrs time it would be night.

65 Rhys

He was trapped in a small space underground by a cave-in, and died two days later.

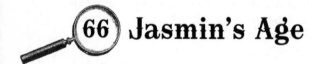

66 Jasmin's Age

Jasmin's age was 22 years and 8 months.

67 John and The Chicken

First determine how far John would travel to catch the chicken if the chicken and John both ran forward on a straight line. Add to this the distance that John would travel to catch the chicken if they ran toward each other on a straight line. Divide the result by 2 and you have the distance that John travels.

In this case, the chicken is 250 yards away, and the speeds of John and the chicken are in the proportion of 4 to 3. So, if both ran forward on a straight line, John would travel 1,000 yards to overtake the chicken. If they travelled toward each other, John would travel $4/7$ths of 250, or 142 $6/7$ yards. Adding the two distances and dividing by 2 gives us 571 $3/7$ yards for the distance travelled by John. Since the chicken runs at $3/4$ the speed of John, it will have travelled three quarters of John's distance, or 428 $4/7$ yards.

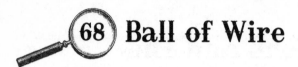

68 Ball of Wire

This problem can be solved with reference to Archimedes' discovery that the volume of a sphere is two-thirds the volume of a cylindrical box into which the sphere exactly fits. The ball of wire has a diameter of 24 inches, so its volume is the same as that of a cylinder with height 16 inches and base diameter 24 inches.

Since wire is simply an extended cylinder, it is necessary to calculate how many pieces of wire 16 inches high and one-hundredth of an inch in diameter, are equal in volume to a 16-inch high cylinder with base diameter of 24 inches. Areas of circles are in the same proportion to each other as the squares of their diameters. The square of 1/100 is 1/10,000, and the square of 24 is 576. Hence the cylinder is equal in volume to 5,760,000 of the 16-inch long wires. The total length of the wire, therefore, is 5,760,000 x 16, or 92,160,000 inches = 1,454 miles and 2,880 feet.

69 Bicycle Rider

The common assumption here is the answer is to halve the total time to obtain the average speed, assuming that the wind boosts the rider's speed in one direction just as much as it retards it in the other direction. This is incorrect, because the wind has helped the rider for only three minutes but has hindered him for four minutes. If he could ride a miles in three minutes with the wind, he could go $1\frac{1}{3}$ miles in four minutes. He returns against the wind in the same four minutes, so he could go $2\frac{1}{3}$ miles in eight minutes, with the wind helping him half the time and hindering him half the time. The wind can therefore be ignored and we conclude that without the wind he could go $2^1/_3$ miles in eight minutes, or one mile in $3^3/_7$ minutes.

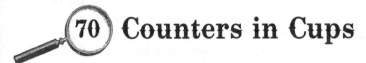

70 Counters in Cups

There is no ordinary way in which the counters can be distributed to solve the problem, so there must be a catch. So there is, and it rests on the ambiguity of how one thing can be placed 'inside' another. The solution requires that one cup be placed inside another.

One solution would be to have three counters in one cup, then six in another cup with one in a second cup inside it.

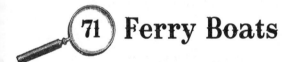

71 Ferry Boats

When the ferry boats meet at point X they are 720 yards from one shore. The combined distance that both have travelled is equal to the width of the river. When they reach the opposite shore, the combined distance is equal to twice the width of the river. On the return trip, they meet at point Y after travelling a combined distance of three times the width of the river, so each boat has gone three times as far as they had when they first met.

At the first meeting, one boat had gone 720 yards, so when it reaches Z it must have gone three times that distance = 2,160 yards. This distance is 400 yards more than the river's width, which must therefore be 2,160 - 400 = 1760 yards or 1 mile wide.

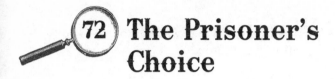

72 The Prisoner's Choice

The prisoner put more green balls than red balls in the first urn, and more red than green in the second. If he were unlucky and chose the second urn, the probability of his drawing a green ball from it would be less than 1/2. He made this probability as close to 1/2 as possible by making the number of red balls in the second urn only one more than the number of green balls, and also by putting in as many balls as possible, i.e. 49 green balls and 50 red balls. He put the remaining green ball in A, and by doing so made drawing a green ball a certainty if he were lucky enough to choose the first urn. Thus his overall probability of success was

$$\frac{1}{2} \times 1 + \frac{1}{2} \times \frac{49}{99} = \frac{74}{99}$$

or a little less than 3/4.

73 Speed of Ant

The ant is approaching Leicester Square Station at 181 inches per second. It doesn't matter how fast the man eats. Since the ant is walking away from his mouth at 1 inch per second, ie 3 inches per second relative to the hot dog, it is moving towards Leicester Square Station 1 inch per second faster than the man is.

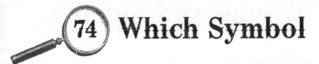

74 Which Symbol

The symbol required is the decimal point, as in 2.3

75 Clock Chimes

Many people assume that they must wait an hour and 45 minutes, until the clock strikes two, before they will know the correct time. In fact, the maximum wait is only an hour and a half, between 12.15 and 1.45, because once the clock has chimed once on seven successive occasions you know that in 15 minutes it will be 2 o'clock.

76 Word Series

The answer is (d) heaven. The sequence of ordinal numbers is implied: first aid, second nature, Third World, Fourth Estate, Fifth Column, sixth sense, seventh heaven.

77 Wayne and Shirley

Most people think that two of each is more likely. But the correct answer is in fact three of one sex and one of the other. Set out below are all the possible combinations of four children:

B	B	B	B		
B	B	B	G	)	
B	B	G	B	)	one
B	G	B	B	)	girl
G	B	B	B	)	
G	G	G	B	)	
G	G	B	G	)	one
G	B	G	G	)	boy
B	G	G	G	)	
B	B	G	G	)	
B	G	B	G	)	
B	G	G	B	)	two of
G	B	B	G	)	each
G	B	G	B	)	
G	G	B	B	)	
G	G	G	G		

Each of the 16 arrangements is equally likely. In eight cases there is a three-one split, whereas in only six cases is there a two-two split.

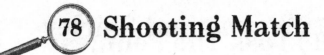

78 Shooting Match

No. Bill and Ben's overall shooting performance was the same. Accuracy ratings are calculated from the ratio of hits to attempts. Bill's rating was 28/84 and Ben's was 25/75, so the two men tied because each hit the target with one third of their shots.

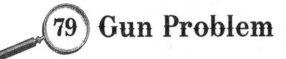

79 Gun Problem

I packed my gun diagonally in a flat square case with sides 1 yard long. The length of the diagonal was the square root of 3, or more than 1.73 yards.

80 Bank Account

There is no reason whatever why the customer's original deposit of £100 should equal the total of the balances left after each withdrawal. The total of withdrawals in the left-hand column must always equal £100, but it is purely coincidence that the total of the right-hand column is close to £100. This is demonstrated by the following example, showing a different pattern of withdrawals:

Withdrawals	Balance left
£5	£95
£5	£90
£90	0
£100	£185

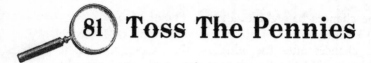

81 Toss The Pennies

No, it would be very unwise of Jack to accept the bet. To find the chances that the three coins will fall alike or not alike, consider all the possible ways that the three coins call fall, as follows:

H	H	H
H	H	T
H	T	H
H	T	T
T	H	H
T	H	T
T	T	H
T	T	T

Each of the eight possibilities is equally likely to occur. Note that only two of them show all the coins alike. This means that the chances of all three coins being alike are two out of eight, or one quarter. There are six ways that the coins can fall without being all alike. Therefore the chances that this will happen are three-quarters.

In other words, Jill would expect in the long run to win three times out of every four tosses. For these wins Jack would pay her £1.50. For the one time that Jack would win, she would pay him £1. This gives Jill a profit of 50p for every four tosses on average.

82 Counter Colours

Most people think that because the state of the bag after the removal of the white counter is exactly the same as it was before the white counter was put in, the probability must be ½. This however is not the case.

The chances before the addition that the bag contains (a) 1 white, and (b) 1 black, are (a) ½, and (b) ½. Hence the chances after the addition, that it contains (a) 2 white, and (b) 1 white + 1 black, are the same: (a) ½ and (b) ½. Now the probabilities which these two states give to the observed event of drawing a white counter are (a) certainty, and (b) ½. Hence the chances, after drawing the white counter, that the bag, before drawing, contained (a) 2 white, and (b) 1 white + 1 black, are proportional to (a) ½ . 1, and (b) ½ . ½; ie (a) ½, and (b) ¼; ie (a) 2, and (b) 1. Hence the chances are (a) two-thirds, and (b) one-third. Hence, after the removal of a white counter, the chances that the bag now contains (a) 1 white or (b) 1 black, are (a) two-thirds, and (b) one-third. Thus the chance of now drawing a white counter is two-thirds.

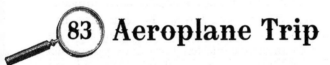

(83) Aeroplane Trip

It is true that the wind increases the plane's speed in one direction by the same amount that it decreases the speed in the other direction. But it is not correct to say that the wind will not affect the plane's average speed for the entire round trip.

Consider the length of time that the plane flies at each of the two speeds. The return trip against the wind will take much longer than the trip with the wind. As a result, more time is spent in flying at the reduced ground speed, and so the average ground speed for both trips will be less than if there were no wind. The stronger the wind, the greater this reduction will be. When the speed of the wind equals or exceeds the plane's speed, then the average ground speed for the round trip becomes zero because the plane is unable to return.

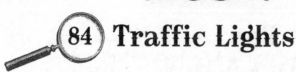

84 Traffic Lights

The answer is 1/8, 1/4, 3/8, 1/4, 1/8 miles.

Since Robert travelled through the whole system in less than two minutes, the total distance is less than two and a half miles, and no section is longer than one and three-quarters miles. If we chart the three arrival times at all possible positions of the first light (green from 3-16 seconds, 29-42 seconds, *etc.*), the only one allowing all three to pass is 1/8 mile:

First Light	Arrival time at 30mph	Arrival time at 50mph	Arrival time at 75mph
1/8	15 sec.	9 sec.	6 sec.
1/4	30 sec.	18 sec. (RED)	
3/8	45 sec. (RED)		
1/2	60 sec.	36 sec.	24 sec. (RED)
5/8	75 sec. (RED)		
3/4	90 sec.	54 sec. (RED)	

Robert arrives at the last light just as it changes. A table of each one-eighth miles together with the light sequence times of traffic lights should they be situated there, shows that the only distance where a light change coincides with Robert's arrival is one and a quarter miles after the start. (For example, a light at a quarter mile after the start would have green showing 15 seconds later than at the first light, and a light at three-eighths of a mile would have green showing 30 seconds later, and so on.)

The same chart shows that, as Robert is not stopped, there is no light at one quarter, five-eighths or one mile from the start. The information about Hubert enables the rest of the distances to be calculated.

85 A Boy, A Girl And A Dog

The dog can be at any point between the boy and the girl, facing either way. To prove this, at the end of one hour place the dog anywhere between the boy and the girl, facing in either direction. Reverse all the motions, and all three will return at the same instant to the starting point.

86 Hat In The River

Because the rate of flow of the river has the same effect on both the boat and the hat, it can be ignored. Instead of the water moving and the shore remaining fixed, imagine the water as perfectly still and the shore moving. As far as the boat and the hat are concerned, this situation is exactly the same as before. Since the man rows 5 miles away from the hat, then 5 miles back, he has rowed a total distance of 10 miles with respect to the water. Since his rowing speed with respect to the water is 5 miles an hour, it must have taken him 2 hours to go the 10 miles. He would therefore recover his hat at 4 o'clock.

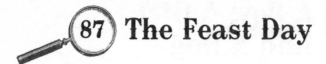

87 The Feast Day

Assume there are N days between consecutive Feast Days, that the temple bell rings every x minutes, and the monastery bell rings every x + p minutes. Since the two bells alternate, the situation is as follows:

The pauses between successive rings are p, 2p, 3p, ..., 3p, 2p, p. Since one of these is one minute, it follows that p = 1. Since the first temple bell is one minute after the monastery bell, the second temple bell is 2 minutes after the monastery bell, and the xth temple bell is x minutes after the xth monastery bell.

Therefore, in the N x 24 x 60 minutes between Feast Days, there are exactly x intervals of x + 1 minutes. Hence x(x + 1) = 1440 x N.

The problem is therefore to find a prime number N such that 1440 x N is the product of two consecutive integers. The obvious candidates are N = 1439 and N = 1441, and indeed 1439 is prime. Hence the answer is 1439 days.

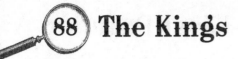

88 The Kings

Let the six cards be numbered 1 to 6, and assume that the two kings are cards 5 and 6. Now list all the different combinations of two cards that can be picked from six, as follows:

1-2	2-3	3-4	4-5	5-6
1-3	2-4	3-5	4-6	
1-4	2-5	3-6		
1-5	2-6			
1-6				

Note that the kings (cards 5 and 6) appear in 9 out of the 15 pairs. Since each pair is equally likely, this means that in the long run a king will be turned up in 9 out of every 15 tries. So the chances of getting a king are three-fifths. This of course is better than one-half, so the answer is that (a) is more likely.

89 The Clock Mender

The answer is 9.48 am on the previous Monday.

We know from the question that the period of observation must be less than eight days, and since the two clocks are known to be keeping different times and gaining or losing less than 60 minutes per day, they cannot both be gaining or both losing for the faster clock could not overtake the slower clock by 12 hours in so short a period. Hence one clock must be gaining by, say, X minutes per day, and the other losing by, say, Y minutes per day. Thus after a true elapsed time of M minutes, the two clocks will have moved forward respectively by the minutes shown below.

$$M \times \frac{1440 + X}{1440} \quad \text{and} \quad M \times \frac{1440 - Y}{1440}$$

For both to show the same hour, the difference between these two movements must equal 12 hours or some multiple thereof, ie:

$$\frac{M(X + Y)}{1440} = 720 \text{ etc.} \quad \text{or} \quad M = \frac{720 \times 1440}{(X + Y)} \text{ etc.}$$

Since M is known to be an integer and less than 8 x 1440 minutes, (X + Y) must be a factor of 720 x 1440, which exceeds 90 but is less than 120, since X, Y are each less than 60. The only such factors are 96, 100 and 108.

If (X + Y) were 96, the true elapsed time, M, would be 10,800 minutes, or 7 days plus 12 hours, which would have terminated outside the clock-mender's working hours so the coincidence of the clocks would have been unobserved. Similarly if (X + Y) were 108, the true elapsed time would be 9,600 minutes or 6 days plus 16 hours, which again would have terminated outside working hours, since 5.00 pm to 9.30 am is already 16½ hours. Thus (X + Y) can only be 100, giving a true elapsed time of 7.2 x 1440 minutes, or 7 and one-fifth days. Since both clocks have moved forward an exact number of minutes, both X and Y must therefore be multiples of 5.

The alternatives, therefore, for the clock which is gaining are 55, 50 or 45 minutes per day, corresponding to gains over the period of 6 hours 36 minutes, 6 hours, and 5 hours 24 minutes respectively, or total forward movements of (7 days plus) 11 hours 24 minutes, 10 hours 48 minutes and 10 hours 12 minutes respectively. Since the clocks were showing a time of 8 o'clock, these movements correspond with original setting times of 8.36, 9.12 and 9.48, of which only 9.48 the previous Monday morning lies within the clock-mender's working hours.

90 Red White Blue

There are twelve possible pairings of the four balls, since you have to treat the two red balls separately. We know that the neither W the B or B then W has been drawn. This leaves ten possible combinations remaining. Only two of those – R1, R2 and R2, R1 – involve two red balls. So the chance is two out of ten, or $^{1}/_{5}$th.

Many people cannot accept that the solution is not 1 in 3, and of course it would be if the balls had been drawn out separately and the colour of the first ball announced as red before the second had been drawn out. However, as both balls had been drawn together, and then the colour of one of the balls announced, then the above solution, 1 in 5, must be correct.

91 Qualifications

Deducting ten, we have 90 applicants who have taken one or two courses. Eighty-three have studied computer science, leaving seven who could have only taken engineering. Deduct these from 75 and we are left with 68 who must have taken both subjects.

92 Common Factor

Each word contains three consecutive letters from the alphabet.

93 Word Groups

The word DUNE from Group 2 belongs best with the words from Group 1, all of which may be preceded by the word 'sand'.

94 The Commuter

A one-way trip by car must take 10 minutes. Therefore walking to the station will take 50 minutes, and walking both ways 100 minutes, or one hour and 40 minutes.

95 Crossing The Desert

Each man will have: 2 full bottles, 1 half-full bottle, and 2 empty bottles.

Reasoning: There is enough water for 7½ full bottles. There are 15 bottles altogether. Therefore each man will end up with 2½ full bottles and 2½ empty bottles. However, half an empty bottle is the same as half a full bottle, leading to the above result.

96 The Cookie Jar

While this is ostensibly a `trial-and-error' exercise, a systematic approach is possible. Specifically, since one child accuses another, and the accused child denies the accusation, one of those statements must be true; they can't both be lies.

Of the statements that remain, only one makes a definite accusation when taken as a lie – Lisa's statement.

So Fred is telling the truth, and Lisa is guilty.

97 A Deck of Cards

Yes it is, because the probability that at least one card will be dealt as it is named is almost 2/3.

98 Two Wins

If Bill is to win two games in a row, he must win the second game, so it is to his advantage to play that game against the weaker opponent. He must also win at least once against the stronger opponent, his father, and his chances of doing so are greater if he plays his father twice. The first game should therefore be against his father.

99 The Lawyers

We have to assume that the agreement was drawn up by a competent lawyer. If so, Protagoras has no cause of action and he cannot succeed. As to the pupil's undertaking to pay if and when he wins a case, by any reasonable interpretation it must be implied that payment for tuition should come from the first fees received. As the pupil was acting for himself, receiving no fees, he would not have to pay.

100 Find X

If each side is squared:

$$X + \sqrt{X + \sqrt{X + \sqrt{X...}}} = 4$$

and if, as stated:

$$\sqrt{X + \sqrt{X + \sqrt{X...}}} = 2$$

then X + 2 = 4, so X = 2.

101 A Piece of Land

If the globe is regarded as exactly spherical, the land that Jason wants is bounded by two meridians and two parallel circles. Imagine the two fixed meridians and a parallel circle moving away from the equator: the arc of the moving parallel intercepted by the two fixed meridians is steadily shortened. The centre of the land that Jason wants should be on the equator. He therefore cannot buy it in England.

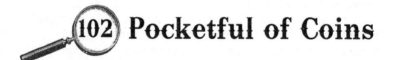

102 Pocketful of Coins

The lowest number of pound coins in a pocket is 0. The next greater number is at least 1, the next greater at least 2, and so on until the number in the tenth pocket is at least 9. Therefore the number of coins required is at least:

$$0 + 1 + 2 + 3 + 4 + 5 + 6 + 7 + 8 + 9 = 45$$

The answer is therefore no – Freddy has only 44 pounds.

103) Gallons

The problem would become simple if you could reduce 3 gallons from the full container A. You can do so only if container B contains 1 gallon. This is easy:
1) Fill A
2) Pour 4 gallons into B
3) 5 gallons remain in A
4) Empty B
5) Refill from A - this leaves 1 gallon in A
6) Empty B and put the 1 gallon from A into B.

104) A Flock of Geese

We know each goose was sold for the same number of pounds as there were geese in the flock. If the number of geese is n, the total number of pounds received was n^2. This was paid in £10 notes plus an excess of less than 10 pound coins. Since George drew both the first and last notes, the total amount must contain an odd number of tens, and since the square of any multiple of 10 contains an even number of tens, n must end in a digit, the square of which contains an odd number of tens. Only two digits, 4 and 6, have such squares: 16 and 36. Both squares end in 6, so n^2 is a number ending in 6. Thus the excess amount consisted of six pound coins.

After Guy took the £6, he still had £4 less than George, so to even things up the older brother wrote out a cheque for £2.

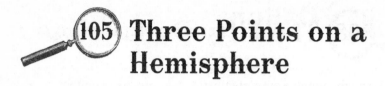

105 Three Points on a Hemisphere

The probability is 1 (complete certainty). Any three points on a sphere must be on a hemisphere.

106 The Bicycle Race

12 minutes.

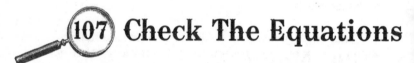

107 Check The Equations

a) Correct
b) 4 / ½ = 8
c) Correct
d) Correct
e) -10(6 - 6) = 0
f) 1/0 = ∞ (The smaller the denominator, the larger the fraction tending to infinity.)
g) Inversely 1/∞ = 0 (Tending to zero.)

(108) The Fifty-Dollar Note

Since the same counterfeit note was used in all the transactions, they are all invalid. Therefore everybody stands in relation to his/her debtor exactly where he/she was before the banker picked up the note, except that the butcher owes, in addition, $50 to the farmer for the calf.

(109) Multiplication

The answer is 0, and it can be arrived at almost instantaneously.

(110) North Pole

If West and East were stationary points, and West on your left when advancing towards North, then after passing the Pole and turning around, West would be on your right. But West and East are not fixed points, but directions round the globe. So wherever you stand facing North you will have the West direction on your left and the East on your right.

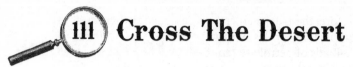

111 Cross The Desert

Let 500 miles be called one 'unit', and the petrol required to travel one unit, a 'load'.

Two loads will carry the lorry a maximum distance of 1 and 1/3 units. This is done in four trips by first setting up a refuelling point 1/3 of a unit from the start. The lorry begins with a full load, goes to the refuelling point, leaves 1/3 load, returns, picks up another full load, arrives at the refuelling point and picks up the 1/3 load. It now has a full load, sufficient to take it the remaining distance to one unit.

Three loads will carry the lorry 1 and 1/3 plus 1/5 units in a total of nine trips. The first refuelling stop is 1/5 unit from the start. Three trips put 6/5 loads in the refuelling station. The truck returns, picks up the remaining full load and arrives at the first stop with 4/5 load in its tank. This, together with the fuel in the cache, makes 1/3 units.

We need to know the minimum amount of fuel for a 800-mile journey. Three loads will take it 766 and 2/3 miles (1 and 1/3 plus 1/5 units), so we need a third cache at a distance of 33 and 1/3 miles (1/15 unit) from the start. In five trips the truck can build up this cache so that when it reaches the cache at the end of the seventh trip, the combined fuel of lorry and cache will be three loads. This is sufficient to take the lorry the remaining distance of 766 and 2/3 miles. Seven trips are made between starting point and first cache, using 7/15 load of petrol. The three loads of fuel that remain are just sufficient for the rest of the way, so the total amount of petrol consumed will be 3 and 7/15 or just over 3.46 loads. Sixteen trips are required.

Similarly, four loads will take the lorry a distance of 1 and 1/3 plus 1/5 plus 1/7 units, with three caches located at the boundaries of these distances. The sum of this infinite series diverges as the number of loads increases.

Therefore, the truck can cross a desert of any width. If the desert is 1,000 miles across, seven caches, 64 trips and 7.673 loads of petrol are required.

The general solution is given by the formula:

$$d = m(1 + 1/3 + 1/5 + 1/7 + ...)$$

where d is the distance to be traversed and m is the number of miles per load of petrol. The number of depots to be established is one less than the number of terms in the series needed to exceed the value of d. One load of petrol is used in the travel between each pair of stations. Since the series is divergent, any distance can be reached by this method, although the amount of petrol needed increases exponentially.

If the lorry is to return eventually to its home station, the formula becomes:

$$d = m(1/2 + 1/4 + 1/6 + 1/8 + ...)$$

This series is also divergent and the solution has properties similar to those for the one-way trip.

(112) Return The Bottle

5p. Let the water = W and the bottle = B:
W + B = 25 and W = 15 + B
So (15 + B) + B = 25, 15+2B=25, and 2B=10.
Therefore B = 5. The water is 15p *more*, not 15p.

(113) Card Games

Nine. Jack wins three games and thus gains £3. Jill has to win back these £3, which takes another three games, and then win three more games to win the total sum of £3.

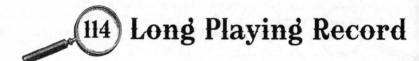

114 Long Playing Record

The answer is about 3 inches. The needle moves from the outermost groove to the innermost groove in an arc whose radius is the length of the pickup arm.

115 Cash Bags

The ten bags should contain the following amounts: £1, £2, £4, £8, £16, £32, £64, £128, £256, £489.

116 Garage Space

Let the number of lorries be X. Then the garage had room for (X - 8) lorries. By increasing the garage by 50 percent there was room for (X + 8) lorries.

$$(X - 8) + \frac{(X - 8)}{2} = X + 8$$
$$3(X - 8)^2 = 2(X + 8)$$
$$3X - 24 = 2X + 16$$
$$\therefore X = 40$$

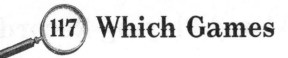

117 Which Games

My friend who does not play rugby does not play football either, and he also does not play cricket. Since he does not play any of the three games, my other two friends play all three games.

118 What Day is it?

Today is Sunday.
Choose a day at random, say Tuesday, then:
1) When the day after tomorrow (ie Thursday) is yesterday (Monday), four days will have elapsed.
2) When the day before yesterday (Sunday) is tomorrow (Wednesday), three days will have elapsed.
3) Today will therefore be seven days from Sunday, i.e. a Sunday.

119 Bag of Sweets

	Joan	Jane	Jill
	4 Sweets	3 sweets	$2^2/_3$
or	12 sweets	9 sweets	14 sweets
Total	264	198	308
Ages	6	4½	7

120 Lost

Stand up the signpost so that the arm which indicates the place I have come from is pointing in the correct direction. All the other arms will then be pointing in the correct directions too.

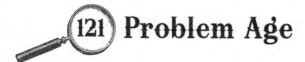

121 Problem Age

This statement was made on 1st January. Peter's birthday is 31st December. He was 17 the day before yesterday. He was 18 yesterday, his birthday. He will be 19 this year, and 20 next year.

122 Panama Canal

The west end of the Panama Canal is in fact in the Caribbean, and the east end in the Pacific. The confusion arises because the isthmus curves around at that point. As can be seen from any atlas, the canal runs from north-west (the Caribbean), to south-east (the Pacific).

123 The Shortcut

At 40 mph. The train would enter the tunnel when John was still two-eighths from the exit or a quarter of the tunnel's length. If the train was to reach him at the exit, it would have to travel at four times John's speed, i.e. 40 mph.

124 How Many Coins

The lowest number of coins is 9, made up as follows: 4 cents, 1 nickel (1 x 5 cents), 2 dimes (2 x 10 cents), 1 quarter (1 x 25 cents), 1 half dollar (1 x 50 cents).

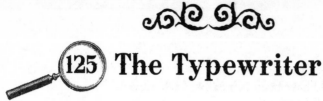

125 The Typewriter

Since none of the letters is in the same row as before, the answer has to be 1 3 1 2 2 2 2 3 2 1.

The old keyboard layout was:

Row 1: **Q W E R T Y U I O P**
Row 2: **A S D F G H J K L**
Row 3: **Z X C V B N M**

The new keyboard layout is:

Row 1: **K***[d]* **C***[e]* **L***[f]* **A***[f]* **G***[f]* **V***[g]* **F***[k]* **N***[k]* **X***[l]* **J***[l]*
Row 2: **B***[a]* **E***[a]* **R***[a]* **P***[h]* **I***[h]* **W***[d,j]* **Y***[d,j]* **Z***[l]* **M***[l]*
Row 3: **S***[b]* **T***[b]* **O***[b]* **U***[b]* **H***[c]* **D***[i]* **Q***[j]*

The letters in square brackets indicate which of the following clues can be used to deduce the positions of the letters on the new keyboard.

a) **BEER** (1 row)
   Old positions: 3 1 1 1
   So on the new keyboard, all must be in row 2.

b) **STOUT** (1 row)
   Old positions: 2 1 1 1 1
   So on the new keyboard, all must be in row 3.

c) **SHERRY** (2 rows)
   Old positions: 2 2 1 1 1 1
   New possibilities are 3 3 2 2 2 (2 or 3).
   H could have been in row 1 or row 3, but since only rows 2 and 3 can be used, H must be in row 3.

d) **WHISKY** (3 rows)
   Old positions: 1 2 1 2 2 1
   New possibilities are (2 or 3) 3 (2 or 3) 3 1 (2 or 3).
   K could have been in row 1 or row 3, but since all three rows must be used, K must be in row 1. At least one of W, I and Y must be in row 2, and any not in row 2 must be in row 3.

e) **HOCK** (2 rows)
   Old positions: 2 1 3 2

New positions are 3 3 1 1.
C could have been 1 or 3, but 3 is barred.

f) **LAGER** (2 rows)
Old positions: 2 2 2 1 1
New positions are 1 1 1 2 2.
L, A and G could have been all in row 1 or all in
row 3, but since there is no room in row 3, they are
all in row 1.

g) **VODKA** (2 rows)
Old positions: 3 1 2 2 2
New positions are 1 3 (1 or 3) 1 1.
V could have been in row 1 or row 2 but only rows
1 and 3 can be used.

h) **CAMPARI** (2 rows)
Old positions: 3 2 3 1 2 1 1
New positions are 1 1 (1 or 2) 2 1 2 2.
P and I could have been in row 2 or row 3, but
only rows 1 and 2 can be used.

i) **CIDER** (3 rows)
Old positions: 3 1 2 1 1
New positions are 1 2 3 2 2.
D must be in row 3 as all three rows must be used.

j) **SQUASH** (2 rows)
Old positions: 2 1 1 2 2 2
New positions are 3 3 3 1 3 3.
Q fills row 3.

k) **FLAGON** (2 rows)
Old positions: 2 2 2 2 1 3
New positions are 1 1 1 1 3 1
F could have been in row 1 or row 3, but 3 is full.
N could have been in row 1 or row 2, but only two
rows can be used.

l) **MUZZY** (2 rows)
Old positions: 3 1 3 3 1
New positions are 2 3 2 2 2.
Thus the remaining letters, X and J, must be in row 1.

My Puzzle Notes